THE ISRA AND MI'RĀJ

THE PROPHET'S NIGHT-JOURNEY AND ASCENT INTO HEAVEN

compiled from *al-Fatḥ al-Bārī*
by 'Abd-Allah Ḥajjāj

translated by Hudā Khaṭṭāb

Dar Al-Taqwa Ltd

SECOND EDITION 1993

ISBN 1870582 063

Translation: Mrs. Huda Khattab

Editorial: Mrs. Jane Kandur & Ms. Zahrah Nicolle

Published by:
Dar Al Taqwa Ltd.
7A Melcombe Street
Baker Street
London
NW1 6AE

Cover design: Hamza Graphics

Printed in Great Britain by:
DELUXE PRINTERS
245A Acton Lane, Park Royal
London NW10 7NR

بسم الله الرحمن الرحيم

CONTENTS

AHĀDĪTH CONCERNING THE ISRĀ' AND MI'RĀJ NARRATED BY BUKHĀRĪ

Jābir ibn 'Abd Allah heard the Prophet (S) say: "When Quraysh disbelieved me (about the Isrā'), I stood up in *al-Ḥijr* (the unroofed part of the *Ka'bah*) and Allah displayed Bayt al-Maqdis to me. So I began to describe its features to them whilst I was looking at it."

Abū Hurayrah said: "On the night in which the Prophet (S) was taken to Jerusalem, he was offered two cups, one containing wine, the other milk. He looked at them, then took the milk. Gabriel said: 'Praise be to Allah Who has guided you towards man's true nature (*Fiṭrah*). If you had taken the wine, your *Ummah* would have gone astray.'"

Mālik ibn Ṣa'ṣa'ah said that the Prophet (S) told him about the night in which he was taken on the Night-Journey. He (S) said: "While I was lying down in *al-Ḥaṭīm* (or *al-Ḥijr*), someone came to me and split open what is between this and this – he indicated the space from the top of his chest to below his navel – and he took out my heart. Then a golden cup filled with faith was brought to me. My heart was washed, filled up (with faith) and put back in its place. A white beast, smaller than a mule, and bigger than a donkey, was brought to me (al-Burāq). One stride of this creature covered a distance as far as it could see. I was mounted upon it.

"Gabriel set off with me until we reached the first heaven, and he asked for it to be opened. He was asked, 'Who is there?' He said, 'Gabriel.' The voice asked, 'Who is with you?' He said, 'Muḥammad.' The voice asked, 'Has revelation been sent to him?' Gabriel answered, 'Yes.' The voice said, 'Welcome to him, blessed is the one who has come' – and the first heaven was opened. When I entered, there was Adam. Gabriel said, 'This is your father Adam; greet him.' I greeted him, and he returned the greeting, then he said, 'Welcome to the righteous son and the righteous Prophet.'

"Then Gabriel took me up until we reached the second heaven, and he asked for it to be opened. He was asked, 'Who is there?' He said, 'Gabriel.' The voice asked, 'Who is with you?' He said, 'Muḥammad.' The voice asked, 'Has revelation been sent to him?' Gabriel answered, 'Yes.' The voice said, 'Welcome to him, blessed is the one who has come' – and the second heaven was opened. When I entered, there were John and Jesus, who were maternal cousins. Gabriel said, 'These are John and Jesus, greet them.' So I greeted them and they returned the greeting. They said, 'Welcome to the righteous brother and the righteous Prophet.'

"Then Gabriel took me up until we reached the third heaven, and he asked for it to be opened. He was asked, 'Who is there?' He said 'Muḥammad.' The voice asked, 'Has revelation been sent to him?' Gabriel answered, 'Yes.' The voice said, 'Welcome to him, blessed is the one who has come' – and the third heaven was opened.

When I entered, there was Joseph. Gabriel said, 'This is Joseph, greet him.' So I greeted him, and he returned the greeting, then he said, 'Welcome to the righteous brother and the righteous Prophet.'

"Then Gabriel took me up until we reached the fourth heaven, and he asked for it to be opened. He was asked, 'Who is there?' He said, 'Gabriel.' The voice asked, 'Who is with you?' He said, 'Muḥammad.' The voice asked, 'Has revelation been sent to him?' Gabriel answered, 'Yes.' The voice said, 'Welcome to him, blessed is he who has come' – and the fourth heaven was opened. When I entered, there was Idrīs. Gabriel said, 'This is Idrīs, greet him.' So I greeted him and he returned the greeting, then he said, 'Welcome to the righteous brother and the righteous Prophet.'

"Then Gabriel took me up until we reached the fifth heaven, and he asked for it to be opened. He was asked, 'Who is there?' He said, 'Gabriel.' The voice asked, 'Who is with you?' He said, 'Muḥammad.' The voice asked, 'Has revelation been sent to him?' Gabriel answered, 'Yes.' The voice said, 'Welcome to him, blessed is he who has come' – and the fifth heaven was opened. When I entered, there was Aaron. Gabriel said, 'This is Aaron, greet him.' So I greeted him and he returned the greeting, then he said, 'Welcome to the righteous brother and the righteous Prophet.'

Then Gabriel took me up until we reached the sixth heaven, and he asked for it to be opened. He was asked, 'Who is there?' He said, 'Gabriel.' The voice asked, 'Who is with you?' He said, 'Muḥammad.' The voice asked, 'Has revelation been sent to him?' Gabriel answered, 'Yes.' The voice said, 'Welcome to him, blessed is he who has come' – and the sixth heaven was opened. When I entered, there was Moses. Gabriel said, 'This is Moses, greet him.' So I greeted him, and he returned the greeting then he said, 'Welcome to the righteous brother and the righteous Prophet.' When I passed by him, he began to weep. He was asked, 'Why do you weep?' He answered, 'I weep because of a young man sent after me, whose *Ummah* will enter Paradise in greater numbers than mine.'

"Then Gabriel took me up to the seventh heaven, and asked for it to be opened. He was asked, 'Who is there?' He said, 'Gabriel.' The voice asked, 'Who is with you?' He said, 'Muḥammad.' The voice asked, 'Has revelation been sent to him?' Gabriel answered, 'Yes.' The voice said, 'Welcome to him, blessed is he who has come' – and the seventh heaven was opened. When I entered, there was Abraham. Gabriel said, 'This is your father, greet him.' So I greeted him, and he returned the greeting then he said, 'Welcome to the righteous son and the righteous Prophet.'

"Then I was taken up to the Lote-tree beyond which none may pass [al-Najm 53:14]. There were four rivers, two hidden and two visible. I asked, 'What is this, O Gabriel?' He said, 'The two hidden rivers are rivers in Paradise. The two visible rivers are the Nile and the Euphrates.'

"Then I was taken up to the 'Much-Frequented House' [al Ṭūr 52:4]. I was presented with three vessels, containing wine, milk and honey. I chose the milk, so Gabriel said, 'This is the natural disposition (*Fiṭrah*) of you and your *Ummah*.'

"Then prayer (*Ṣalāt*) was made obligatory: fifty prayers every day. Then I returned, and passed by Moses, who asked, 'What have you been commanded to do?' I said, 'I have been commanded to perform fifty prayers every day.' He said, 'Your *Ummah* will not be able to perform fifty prayers every day. By Allah, I tested the people before you, and I tried my utmost to reform the people of Israel. Go back to your Lord and ask Him to lighten the burden of your *Ummah*.' So I went back, and the number of prayers was reduced by ten (to forty). I went back to Moses, and he said the same as before. So I went back and the number of prayers was reduced by a further ten (to thirty). I went back to Moses and he said the same as before. So I went back again, and I was commanded to pray five times every day. I came back to Moses, and he asked, 'What have you been commanded to do?' I said, 'To perform five prayers every day.' Moses said, 'Your *Ummah* will not be able to perform five prayers every day. I have tested the people before you, and I tried my utmost to reform the people of Israel. Go back to your Lord and ask Him to lighten the burden of your *Ummah*.' I said, 'I asked my Lord until I felt ashamed. Now I am content and submit (to His Will).' When I passed by, a voice proclaimed, 'I have confirmed My command and lightened the burden of My servants.'"

Another report says: "Whilst I was lying down in the vicinity of the Ka'bah, half-asleep and half-awake, two men came to me. One brought a golden vessel filled with wisdom and faith. He opened up the space between the top of my chest to below my navel, then he washed my heart (lit. = 'stomach') with Zamzam water, and filled it with wisdom and faith."

With reference to the Much-Frequented House, this report adds, "I asked Gabriel about it, and he said, 'Every day, seventy thousand angels pray in it, and when they leave, another seventy thousand come.' He took me up to the Lote-tree beyond which none may pass: its fruits were like the pitchers of Hajar and its leaves were like the ears of elephants . . " The end of this report adds: "It was proclaimed: 'I have confirmed My command, lightened the burden of My servants, and increased the reward (for the prayers) tenfold.'"

With regard to the *Āyah* –

> " . . . We granted the vision which We showed thee, but as a trial for men . . . " (al-Isrā' 17:60)

– Ibn 'Abbās said: "The vision was something which the Prophet (S) actually saw with his physical eyes. It was shown to him on the night when he was taken to Bayt al-Maqdis. 'The Cursed Tree' (mentioned) in the Qur'ān [al-Isrā' 17:60] is the tree of *Zaqqūm* (a tree in Hell which has bitter fruit)."

Abū Dharr reported that the Prophet (S) said: "When I was at Makkah, the roof of my house was opened, and Gabriel descended. He opened my chest, and washed it with Zamzam water. He brought a golden vessel filled with wisdom and faith, poured them into my chest, then closed it up. Then he took my hand and led me up to the first heaven. When I reached the first heaven, Gabriel said to the gatekeeper, 'Open the gate.' The gatekeeper asked, 'Who is there?' He said, 'Gabriel.' The gatekeeper asked, 'Is there anyone with you?' Gabriel said, 'Yes, Muḥammad is with me.' The gatekeeper asked, 'Has revelation been sent to him?' Gabriel said, 'Yes.' When the gate was opened, we passed over the first heaven. We saw a man sitting, with a multitude of people on his right and left. When he looked towards the right, he laughed, and when he looked towards the left, he wept. He said, 'Welcome to the righteous Prophet and the righteous son.' I asked, 'Who is this?' Gabriel answered, 'This is Adam, and the multitudes on his right and left are the souls of his descendants. Those on his right are the people of paradise, those on his left are the people of Hell. So when he looks to his right, he laughs, and when he looks to his left, he weeps.'

"Then Gabriel took me up to the second heaven, and said to its gatekeeper, 'Open the gate.' The gatekeeper asked him the same questions as the first gatekeeper, and received the same replies, then he opened the gate."

Abū Dharr added that the Prophet (S) met Adam, Idris, Moses, Jesus and Abraham, but he did not mention in which heavens they were, apart from stating that the Prophet (S) met Adam in the first heaven, and Abraham in the sixth heaven.

Anas said: "When Gabriel brought the Prophet (S) past Idrīs, the latter said, 'Welcome to the righteous Prophet and the righteous brother.' The Prophet (S) asked, 'Who is this?' Gabriel said, 'This is Idrīs.' Then he passed by Moses, who said, 'Welcome to the righteous Prophet and the righteous brother.' The Prophet (S) asked, 'Who is this?' Gabriel answered, 'This is Moses.' Then he passed by Jesus, who said, 'Welcome to the righteous Prophet and the righteous brother.' The Prophet (S) asked, 'Who is this?' Gabriel answered, 'This is Jesus.' Then he passed by Abraham, who said, 'Welcome to the righteous Prophet and the righteous son.' The Prophet (S) asked, 'Who is this?' Gabriel answered, 'This is Abraham, upon whom be peace.'"

The Prophet (S) added, "Then Gabriel took me up to a place where I heard the creaking of the pens."

Ibn Ḥazm and Anas ibn Malik reported that the Prophet (S) said: "Allah enjoined fifty prayers on my *Ummah*. When I was returning with this commandment,

I passed by Moses, who asked me, 'What has Allah enjoined upon your *Ummah*?' I said, 'He has enjoined fifty prayers.' Moses said, 'Go back to your Lord, for your *Ummah* will not be able to bear it.' So I went back to my Lord, and He reduced the number of prayers by half. I went back to Moses, and said, 'It has been reduced by half.' Moses said, 'Go back to your Lord, for your *Ummah* will not be able to bear it.' So I went back, and the number was reduced by half again. I returned to Moses, and again he said, 'Go back to your Lord, for your *Ummah* will not be able to bear it.' So I went back to Him, and He said, 'They are five prayers but they are equal in reward to fifty, for My word does not change.' I returned to Moses, who said, 'Go back to your Lord again.' But I said, 'I feel ashamed to ask my Lord again.' Then Gabriel took me up as far as the Lote-tree, beyond which none may pass; it was veiled in colours indescribable. Then I was granted admission to Paradise, where I saw nets made of pearls, and its earth was of musk."

Sharīk ibn 'Abd Allah said: 'I heard Anas ibn Malik say: "On the night of the Isrā' when the Prophet (S) was taken from the *Ka'bah*, three people came to him before revelation was sent to him, whilst he was sleeping in *Masjid al-Ḥarām* (the Mosque at Makkah). The first of them said, 'Which one is he?' The middle one said, 'He is the best of them.' One of them said, 'Take the best of them.' That night they did no more. They came back to take him on another night, which is when he saw them whilst his heart was awake, and could see although his eye slept, for this is a characteristic of all Prophets; whilst their eyes sleep their hearts are awake and aware. They did not speak to him, but carried him to the well of Zamzam. Gabriel was in charge of them, and he split open the Prophet's (S) chest. Then he washed it with Zamzam water until his heart was made pure. Then he brought a golden vessel, full of faith and wisdom, and emptied it into his heart until it overflowed. Then Gabriel closed up his chest and took him up to the first heaven, where he knocked on one of its gates.

"The people of the first heaven asked, 'Who is there?' He said, 'Gabriel.' They asked, 'Who is with you?' Gabriel said, 'Muḥammad is with me.' They asked, 'Has revelation been sent to him?' Gabriel said, 'Yes.' They said, 'Then welcome to him, welcome.' They welcomed him joyfully, although the people of heaven do not know what Allah wills on earth until He informs them. The Prophet (S) found Adam in the first heaven. Gabriel said, 'This is your father, greet him.' So the Prophet (S) greeted him, and Adam returned the greeting, then said, 'Welcome O my son, and what an excellent son you are!'

"There were two rivers running through the first heaven. The Prophet (S) asked, 'What are these rivers, O Gabriel?' Gabriel answered, 'They are the essence of the Nile and Euphrates.' Then Gabriel took him through the first heaven, where they saw another river, above which stood a castle made of pearls and chrysolite. The Prophet (S) struck it with his hand, and found that it was pungent musk; he asked, 'What is this, O Gabriel?' Gabriel answered, 'This is *al-Kawthar*, which your Lord is keeping for you.'

"Then Gabriel took him up to the second heaven, where the angels asked similar questions to those asked by the angels in the first heaven. They asked, 'Who is there?' Gabriel said, 'Gabriel.' The angels asked, 'Who is with you?' Gabriel answered, 'Muḥammad.' They asked, 'Has revelation been sent to him?' Gabriel said, 'Yes.' so they said, 'Then welcome to him.'

"Then Gabriel took him up to the third, fourth, fifth, sixth and seventh heavens. In each heaven the angels asked the same questions. In each heaven there were Prophets also. The Prophet (S) named them, and I (i.e. Ibn Malik – the narrator of the *Ḥadīth*) remembered only some of them: Idrīs in the second heaven, Aaron in the fourth, another – whose name I did not remember – in the fifth, Abraham in the sixth and Moses in the seventh, by virtue of the fact that he spoke to Allah. Moses said,

'My Lord, I did not think that You would raise anyone above me.'

"Then Gabriel took him higher, to regions which are unknown to all except Allah, until they reached the Lote-tree, beyond which none may pass. Then Allah the Almighty drew near, until He was very close indeed, and revealed the commandment: 'Fifty prayers, day and night, are prescribed for your *Ummah*.'

"Then the Prophet (S) came back down, until he reached Moses, who stopped him and said, 'O Muhammad, what has your Lord enjoined upon you?' The Prophet (S) said, 'He has enjoined fifty prayers, day and night, upon me.' Moses said, 'Verily your *Ummah* will not be able to bear it. Go back and ask your Lord to lighten the burden for yourself and your *Ummah*.' The Prophet (S) turned to Gabriel, as if asking for advice. Gabriel indicated that he was prepared to go back if that was what the Prophet (S) wanted; so he took him back up. The Prophet (S) said, 'O Lord, lighten our load, for my *Ummah* will not be able to bear it.' So Allah SWT reduced the number of prayers by ten. Then the Prophet (S) went back to Moses, who stopped him again, and sent him back several times until the number of prayers was reduced to five.

"Then Moses stopped him again, and said, 'O Muhammad, I urged my people Bani Israel to do less than this, but they were weak and neglected their duty. Your *Ummah* is weaker in body and heart, sight and hearing. Go back and ask your Lord to lighten the load.' The Prophet (S) again turned to Gabriel for advice; he did not object, and took him back up for the fifth time. The Prophet (S) said, 'O my Lord, my *Ummah* are weak in body and heart, pray lighten our load.' Allah SWT said, 'O Muḥammad.' The Prophet (S) said, 'Here I am at Your service.' Allah SWT said, 'My Word does not change. It must remain as it was decided in the 'Source of Decrees' [*Umm al-Kitāb*; cf. al-Zukhruf 43:4]. Every good deed will have a tenfold reward. The number of prayers prescribed in the Source of Decrees is fifty, but you are obliged to perform only five (as each carries a tenfold reward).'

"The Prophet (S) returned to Moses, who asked, 'What happened?' The Prophet (S) said, 'Allah has lightened our load, and has given us a tenfold reward for every good deed.' Moses said, 'By Allah, I urged Bani Israel to do less than that, and they failed. Go back to your Lord and ask Him to reduce the number still further.' But the Prophet (S) said, 'O Moses, by Allah I feel ashamed before my Lord for disputing with Him.' Moses said, 'Then go down in the name of Allah' . . . Then the Prophet (S) woke up in the Masjid al-Ḥarām."

WHY WAS THE PROPHET (S) TAKEN TO BAYT AL-MAQDIS BEFORE THE ASCENT TO HEAVEN?

Al-Ḥāfiẓ said, Ka'b ibn Aḥbār narrated that the gate of heaven called *Maṣ'ad al-Malā'ikah* ("The angels' point of ascent") faces Bayt al-Maqdis. The *'Ulamā'* understood from this that the reason why the Prophet (S) was taken to Bayt al-Maqdis before the ascent was so that he could be taken straight up. But this opinion needs to be examined further, because of the reports that there is a "Much-Frequented House" in every heaven, and that the one in the first heaven is a reflection of the Ka'bah. In this case it would have seemed more appropriate for the ascent to have taken place from Makkah, so as to reach the House directly, because the Prophet (S) was taken up from one heaven to the next until he reached the Much-Frequented House.

Other, weaker, suggestions have also been put forward. For example: so that the Prophet (S) would see both of the *Qiblahs* on that night; or because Bayt al-Maqdis had been the place to which most of the previous Prophets had migrated, so the Prophet Muhammad (S) had to go there to have the same virtues as they had; or because Jerusalem will be the place of assembly in the Hereafter, and most of the events of that night had more to do with the Hereafter, so it was more appropriate for the Mi'rāj to start from there; or it was so that the Prophets might be gathered together in one place; and Allah knows best.

WERE THE ISRĀ' AND MI'RĀJ A DREAM, OR DID THEY HAPPEN WHILST THE PROPHET (S) WAS AWAKE?

The earliest Muslims differed concerning this matter because the reports differed. Some of them were of the opinion that the Isrā' and Mi'rāj happened in one night, whilst the Prophet (S) was awake, that both his body and soul were taken up, and that this happened after Revelation had been sent to him. This is the opinion favoured by the majority of scholars, specialists in *Ḥadīth* and *Fiqh*, and Islamic philosophers, and is supported by the soundest (*Ṣaḥīḥ*) reports. We should not oppose their opinion as long as it does not go against reason, or require complicated and improbable explanations.

There are indeed some reports which contradict the opinion mentioned above. Some scholars say that the Isrā' and Mi'rāj happened twice: once in a dream, as preparation for the physical ascent, and then when the Prophet (S) was awake; something similar to this happened during the first period of revelation.

The great Tābi'ī Ibn Maysarah and others suggested that the Isrā' and Mi'rāj took place in a dream. They reconcile their opinion with the *Ḥadīth* of 'Ā'ishah by saying that they happened twice. The commentator on Bukhārī, al-Muhallab, quoting from several sources, and Abu Naṣr ibn al-Qushayrī, are also of the same opinion. Abū Sa'īd had suggested it earlier in his book *Sharaf al-Muṣṭafā* where he said: "The Prophet (S) made several ascents, some whilst he was awake and some in dreams." Al-Suhayli reported it from Ibn al-'Arabī, and favoured this report.

Some of those who think that it happened twice suggest that the Isrā' and Mi'rāj which took place in a dream happened before revelation was sent to the Prophet (S). They base this suggestion on the phrase in Sharīk's report from Anas [see p. 11] ". . . before revelation was sent to him . . .", but this phrase was rejected by al-Khaṭṭābī, Ibn Ḥazm, 'Abd al-Haqq, al-Qāḍī 'Ayyaḍ and al-Nawawī. Al-Nawawī said: "In this report of Sharīk's there are errors which the scholars rejected; one of these is the phrase '. . . before revelation was sent to him . . .'" The scholars agree that prayer was enjoined upon the *Ummah* during the night of the Isra', so how could it have occurred before revelation had been sent to the Prophet (S)?

Some later scholars suggested the Isrā' and Mi'rāj took place on two different nights, on the basis of Sharīk's version of the *Ḥadīth* of Anas, which does not mention the Isrā'. The same appears to be the case in the *Ḥadith* of Malik ibn Ṣā'ṣa'ah [see p. 5]. But this does not necessarily imply a number of different nights. It means that some reports mentioned details which others omitted, as we shall explain.

Some scholars suggest that the Isrā' happened whilst the Prophet (S) was awake and that the Mi'rāj took place in a dream, or that the dispute as to whether the Prophet (S) was asleep or awake applies only to the Mi'rāj and not to the Isrā', because when he told Quraysh and they disbelieved him and doubted that such a thing could happen, they did not refer to the Mi'rāj. Also, Allah SWT said:

> "Glory to (God) Who did take His Servant for a journey by night from the Sacred Mosque to the Farthest Mosque . . ." (al-Isrā' 17:1)

If the Mi'rāj had taken place whilst the Prophet (S) was awake, it would have been even more deserving of mention. But it was not mentioned in this *Āyah*, despite the fact that it was more miraculous and far stranger than the Isrā'. This would indicate that it took place in a dream. However, if the Isrā' had taken place in a dream, Quraysh would have had no reason to doubt him, because it is quite likely that any person may see something like this, or even stranger, in a dream.

DID THE ISRĀ' AND MI'RĀJ HAPPEN ON ONE AND THE SAME NIGHT?

It is said that the Isrā' happened twice, and on both occasions the Prophet (S) was awake. On the first occasion, he returned from Bayt al-Maqdis, and in the morning he told Quraysh what had happened. On the second occasion he was taken to Bayt al-Maqdis, then on the same night he was taken up to heaven, where the events mentioned in the reports given above took place. Quraysh did not even bother to argue about this matter. As far as they were concerned it was akin to the Prophet's (S) telling them that the angel came to him from heaven in the twinkling of an eye. They had rejected this as they thought it was impossible, in spite of the miracles which the Prophet (S) had performed to prove his veracity – but they were stubborn and insisted on disbelieving him. But when he told them that he had travelled to Bayt al-Maqdis and returned in one night, they disbelieved him and asked him to describe it, because some of them knew it, and they also knew that he had not seen it before. So in this case, unlike with the Mi'rāj, they could find out for themselves whether he was speaking the truth.

Some reports support the idea that the Mi'rāj happened straight after the Isrā', and that they both took place on one night. Thābit's report from Anas, in *Ṣaḥīḥ Muslim*, begins: "Al-Burāq was brought to me, and I rode on it until I reached Bayt al-Maqdis . . ." The story goes on to say: ". . . Then we were taken up to the first heaven." According to Abu Sa'īd al-Khudrī's *Ḥadīth* in Ibn Isḥāq's book, the Prophet (S) said: "When I had finished what I had to do in Jerusalem, then the Mi'rāj (here = 'ladder') was brought to me . . ." Malik ibn Ṣa'ṣa'ah begins his *Ḥadīth* by saying that the Prophet

(S) told them about the night in which he was taken on the Night-Journey. Even if he does not mention the Night-Journey to Bayt al-Maqdis as such, he refers to it.

Those who argue that the Isrā' took place on its own, and was not immediately followed by the Mi'rāj, base their argument on the report of al-Bazzār and al-Ṭabarānī, which was verified by al-Bayhaqī in *al-Dalā'il*. They quote the *Ḥadīth* of Shaddād ibn Aws who said: "We said: 'O Messenger of Allah, how were you taken on the Night-Journey?' He said: 'I prayed the night prayer in Makkah, then Gabriel brought a creature (*al-Burāq*) to me . . .'" – the *Ḥadith* goes on to mention the journey to Bayt al-Maqdis and what happened there – ". . . Then we went back, and we passed the camels of Quraysh in such-and-such a place . . . Then I came back to my Companions in Makkah before dawn."

If it can be proved that the Mi'rāj happened in a dream, as stated in Sharīk's *Ḥadīth* reported from Anas, then it must follow that the Mi'rāj happened twice: once in a dream as a preparation for the later event, and then when the Prophet (S) was awake, in conjunction with the Isrā'. But the suggestion that it happened before revelation was sent to the Prophet (S) cannot be proved.

Imām Abū Shāmah suggests that the Mi'rāj happened on several occasions. He bases his argument on the *Ḥadīth* which al-Bazzār and Sa'īd ibn Manṣūr narrated, through Abū 'Imran al-Jūnī, from Anas, according to which the Prophet (S) said: "Whilst I was sitting, Gabriel came to me and tapped me on the back. We got up and went to a tree in which were what looked like two birds' nests. I sat in one and Gabriel sat in the other, and the tree rose up until it filled the sky . . . A gate in heaven was opened for me, and I saw the greatest light. It was covered with a curtain made of pearls and sapphires." This *Ḥadīth* refers to another event, which appears to have taken place in Madīnah. It is not impossible for such an event to have taken place, but it is unlikely that the Mi'rāj, in which the Prophet (S) asked about every Prophet, and was asked whether revelation had yet been sent, and in which five daily prayers were enjoined, etc., would have happened more than once. It does not make sense to suggest that these events took place more than once whilst the Prophet (S) was awake, so we must compare the various reports and see which are the most authentic. But it would not be impossible for these events to have happened in a dream, as a form of preparation, and then for the self-same events to have taken place whilst the Prophet (S) was awake, as suggested above.

The word "*Isrā'*" is derived from the Arabic word "*asrā*", which means "to travel at night".

The phrase "(Allah) took His Servant for a Journey by night . . . *(asrā bi 'Abdihi)*" [al-Isrā' 17:1] means that Allah SWT caused *al-Burāq* to carry His Servant on a journey by night. "His Servant" (*'abdihi*) refers to Muḥammad (S) as all scholars agree, and the pronoun "His" refers to Allah SWT. The adverb "by night" (*laylan*) reinforces the meaning of the verb *asrā*, which means "to travel by night" or "to make (someone) travel by night", and shows that it is not being used in any metaphorical sense. Some scholars say this indicates that it happened only in some part of the night, not the whole night.

WHEN DID THE MI'RĀJ HAPPEN?

There are some differences as to when the Mi'rāj took place. Some suggest that it took place before revelation was sent, but this is a very strange suggestion, unless it can be interpreted as saying that the Mi'rāj took place in a dream. The majority of scholars state that it happened after revelation had been sent, but differ as to when it happened. Some say it took place one year before the Hijrah. Ibn Ṣa'd and others favour this opinion, and al-Nawawī was certain of it. Ibn Ḥazm made the exaggerated claim that here was *Ijmā'* (concensus) on this issue, but this claim can be rejected because there is so much dispute over this matter. In fact there are more than ten suggestions, which include the following:

Ibn al-Jawzī said that it happened eight months before the Hijrah; Abū al-Rabī' ibn Sālim said that it was six months before the Hijrah. Ibn Ḥazm stated that it happened in Rajab of the twelfth year of the Prophethood. Ibrāhīm al-Ḥarbī was certain that it was eleven months before the Hijrah, when he said, "It happened in Rabī' al-Ākhir of the year before the Hijrah." Ibn al-Munīr, in his commentary on the *Sīrah* by Ibn 'Abd al-Barr thought this suggestion the most likely. Ibn 'Abd al-Barr himself suggested that it happened one year and two months before the Hijrah. Ibn Faris suggested one year and three months; al-Saddī suggested one year and five months, quoting from al-Ṭabarī and al-Bayhaqī.

According to this last suggestion, it took place in Shawwāl or Ramaḍān. Al-Wāqidī was certain of this, and Ibn Quṭaybah and Ibn 'Abd al-Barr mentioned something similar, namely that it took place eighteen months before the Hijrah. Ibn Ṣa'd, reporting from Ibn Abi Sīrah, also states that it happened in Ramaḍān, eighteen months before the Hijrah.

The phrase "They came back to take him on another night . . ." in the *Ḥadīth* narrated by Sharīk from Anas ibn Mālik [p. 11] does not define the period between the two occasions when the angels came. It is understood that the second occasion was after revelation had been sent, and on that occasion the Isrā' and Mi'rāj took place. But it does not make any difference if the period between the two occasions was one night, several nights or even a number of years. So there is no problem with Sharīk's report, and we can understand that the Isrā' happened whilst the Prophet (S) was awake, after revelation had been sent and before the Hijrah.

The strongest indication that the Mi'rāj happened after revelation had been sent comes in this same *Ḥadīth*, where the gatekeeper of Heaven asks Gabriel if revelation has been sent to Muḥammad (S) yet, and Gabriel replies in the affirmative.

HOW MANY TIMES WAS THE PROPHET'S (S) CHEST SPLIT?

We also know that the Prophet's (S) chest was split at the time of the first revelation. Each time it happened there was a reason and wisdom behind it. The first time it happened was recorded by Muslim in the *Ḥadīth* from Anas which states: "(Gabriel) took out something like a clot of blood and said: 'This is the Shayṭān's share of you.'" This happened when the Prophet (S) was still a child, so he grew up in the best possible way and was protected from the Shayṭān.

His chest was split open again at the time of the first revelation, to honour him further and to make his heart strong and pure in preparation for the revelation which was to come.

The third time it happened was at the time of the Mi'rāj, to prepare the Prophet (S) for his close encounter with Allah SWT. It has been suggested that the wisdom behind this washing was so that the Prophet's (S) chest would have been washed three times, as Muslims were later commanded to wash three times during their ablutions. Others have suggested that the roof of the Prophet's (S) house was split asunder as a portent of the splitting open of his chest, and a sign that no scar would remain.

We should accept everything which has been reported concerning the splitting open of the Prophet's chest, the taking out of his heart and all other extraordinary events. We should not try to explain them away as being metaphorical, because Allah is perfectly able to do such things, and nothing is impossible for Him. Al-Qurṭabī said, in *al-Mufahham*: "No-one should deny that the Prophet's (S) chest was opened on the night of the Isrā', because all the scholars who reported it are well-known and reliable."

AL-BURĀQ

The *Ḥadīth* of Mālik ibn Ṣa'ṣa'ah says of al-Burāq that "One stride of this creature covered a distance as far as it could see" [see p. 5]. Ibn Ṣa'd, reporting from al-Wāqidī, says that al-Burāq had two wings, but this is the only report which mentions this. Al-Tha'labī, in a report with a weak *Isnād* from Ibn 'Abbās says that al-Burāq "Had a cheek like that of a man, a mane like that of a horse, legs like those of a camel, hooves and a tail like those of an ox, and his chest looked like a ruby."

The word "al-Burāq" is related to other Arabic words: *barīq*, meaning white; *barq*, meaning lightening; and *barqa'*, which refers to a sheep which is white with black spots. This last meaning does not contradict the *Ḥadīth* which says that al-Burāq was white, because sheep which are described as *barqā'* are considered white.

Some scholars suggest that "al-Burāq" is not related to these other words – it is a unique name referring to a unique creature, because there is no report of anybody owning it – in contrast to the situation of other similar animals. Allah SWT could have caused the Prophet (S) to ascend without the aid of al-Burāq, but by making him ride al-Burāq, He honoured him more, because if the Prophet (S) had ascended by himself, that would have been like walking, and it is nobler to ride than to walk.

With regard to the expression "I was mounted upon it" [in Ibn Ṣa'ṣa'ah's report, p. 5], according to a report given by Abū Sa'īd in *Sharaf al-Muṣṭafa*, "The one who held the stirrup was Gabriel and the one who held the reins of al-Burāq was Michael." Muammar transmitted a report from Qutādah, who transmitted it from Anas, which said: "On the night of the Isrā', al-Burāq was brought, saddled and bridled, to the Prophet (S). Al-Burāq shied, but Gabriel said to him, 'Why are you doing this? By Allah, no-one more honoured by Allah than this man has ever ridden you.' At that, al-Burāq began to sweat." (Reported by Tirmidhī, who considered it to be *Ḥasan Gharīb*; Ibn Ḥibbān considered it to be *Ṣaḥīḥ*.)

Ibn Isḥāq narrated from Qutādah: "When al-Burāq shied, Gabriel put his hand on his mane and asked, 'Are you not ashamed . . . ?'" Wathīmah narrated from Ibn Isḥāq: "Al-Burāq trembled and sank to the ground. Then I rode upon it." Another, similar report narrated from Anas, adds: "Al-Burāq was used by the Prophets before Muḥammad (S)."

This indicates that al-Burāq was created for the Prophets to ride. Al-Suhaylī suggests that when al-Burāq shied away, it was because such a long time had elapsed since it had last been ridden by any Prophet. Al-Nawawī, quoting from al-Zubayrī in *Mukhtaṣar al-'Aynī*, said: "The Prophets used to ride al-Burāq" – but some suggested that this idea needed the support of an authentic report.

However, there are some authentic reports, for example the report which says: "I tied al-Burāq up at the same hitching-post which had been used by the earlier prophets." Ibn Isḥāq, in *al-Mubtadā'*, mentions a report from Wathīmah concerning the Isrā': "Al-Burāq shied away. The Prophets before me had ridden it, but that had been long before, and no-one had ridden it in the period since the time of Jesus." In *Maghāzī Ibn 'Ā'idh*, a report of al-Zuhrī, from Sa'īd ibn al-Musayyab, says: "Al-Burāq: the beast on which Abraham used to visit Ishmael."

Abū Ya'lā and al-Ḥākim reported from the *Ḥadīth* of Ibn Mas'ūd: "Al-Burāq was brought to me, and I rode on it behind Gabriel."

These reports indicate that al-Burāq was ridden by others.

Ibn al-Munīr said: "When al-Burāq shied away, it was because it felt so proud and happy that the Prophet (S) was to ride it. Gabriel wanted al-Burāq to explain why he shied away, so he began to sweat because of that.

A similar thing happened when the mountain of Uḥud shook, until the Prophet (S) said to it: "Be still: there are a Prophet, a *Siddīq* and martyr upon you" – the mountain was trembling with joy, not anger.

THE PROPHET'S (S) ARRIVAL IN THE FIRST HEAVEN

Some reports say "Gabriel set off with me" whilst others say, "I set off with Gabriel". However, there is no difference between them, contrary to the opinion of some who say that the second phrase indicates that the Prophet (S) did not need Gabriel for the ascent, but that they were equals. But the majority of reports use the first phrase. In the *Ḥadīth* of Abū Dharr, narrated by Bukhārī at the beginning of *Kitāb al-Ṣalāt* (The Book of Prayer), he says: "Then Gabriel took my hand and ascended with me." This indicates that at that stage, Gabriel was a guide for the Prophet (S).

The phrase "Until we reached the first heaven" would seem to indicate that the Prophet (S) stayed on al-Burāq until he ascended to heaven. Those who claim that the Mi'rāj took place on a different night than the Isrā' adhere to this report. According to reports other than that of Malik ibn Ṣa'ṣa'ah, the Prophet (S) did not ascend on al-Burāq, but by means of the Mi'rāj, which is a ladder or stairway, as was clearly stated in the *Ḥadīth* of Abū Sa'īd, narrated from Ibn Isḥāq and al-Bayhaqī in *al-Dalā'il*, which says: "I was brought a beast like a mule, with big ears, which was called al-Burāq. The Prophets before me had ridden it, and I rode it too . . . Then Gabriel and I entered Bayt al-Maqdis, where I prayed. Then the Mi'rāj was brought to me."

According to a report given by Ibn Isḥāq: "I heard the Prophet (S) say: 'When I had finished what I had to do in Bayt al-Maqdis, the Mi'rāj was brought to me. I had never seen anything more beautiful than it. This is what the deceased looks at when he dies. My companion (Gabriel) took me up on it until we reached one of the gates of heaven.'"

According to a report given by Ka'b: "Steps of silver and gold were placed before them until he and Gabriel reached the top." A report given by Abū Sa'īd in *Sharaf al-Muṣṭafā*: "The Mi'rāj was brought to him from *Jannat al-Firdaws*. It was adorned with pearls, and there were angels on its right and left."

The *Ḥadīth* of Abū Sa'īd narrated by al-Bayhaqī says: ". . . I reached Bayt al-Maqdis, where I tied my beast (al-Burāq) up to the hitching-post which all the Prophets before me had used . . . Gabriel and I entered Bayt al-Maqdis where we both prayed two Rak'ahs." Abū 'Ubaydah ibn 'Abd Allah ibn Mas'ūd related a similar report from his father, and added: "Then I entered the Mosque, where I saw all the Prophets praying – some standing, some bowing and some prostrating. Then the *Iqāmah* (second call to prayer) was given, and I led them in prayer." Yazīd ibn Abī Mālik's report from Anas, narrated by Ibn Abī Ḥātim, says: "It was not long before many people had gathered. Then the Muezzin gave the call to prayer (*Adhān*) and the second call (*Iqāmah*). So we stood up in rows, waiting to see who would lead us in prayer. Then Gabriel took me by the hand and led me to the front, so I led them in prayer." The *Ḥadīth* of Ibn Mas'ūd in Muslim's *Ṣaḥīḥ* says: "The time for prayer came, and I led them in prayer." The *Ḥadīth* of Ibn 'Abbās narrated by Aḥmad says: "When the Prophet (S) reached al-Masjid al-Aqṣā, he began to pray. The Prophets gathered and prayed with him." Another *Ḥadīth* narrated by Aḥmad tells us that when 'Umar entered Bayt al-Maqdis, he said: "I shall pray where the Prophet (S) prayed" – then he went forward to the Qiblah and prayed.

'Ayāḍ said: "It is possible that he prayed with all the Prophets in Bayt al-Maqdis, then ascended to heaven. It is also possible that he prayed with them after descending from heaven, and that they descended too." Another scholar said: "His seeing the Prophets in heaven could mean that he saw their souls – except for Jesus, who is known to have been taken up bodily; and something similar is said with regard to Idrīs too. Those who prayed with him in Bayt al-Maqdis may have been there as souls only, or in body and soul. It is more likely that he prayed with them in Bayt al-Maqdis before the ascent; but Allah knows best."

There are several opinions as to why the Prophet (S) met only some of the previous Prophets. Al-Suhaylī suggests that the meeting with these particular Prophets foreshadowed events which would happen in the life of the Prophet Muḥammad (S).

With Adam, one can see a similarity between Adam's leaving Paradise and descending to earth, and the Hijrah to Madīnah. Both of them did not like to leave their former abode, but the destiny of both was to return there.

With Jesus and John, the similarity is the hostility of the Jews which the Prophet Muḥammad (S) encountered at the beginning of the Hijrī period, when they were unjust in the extreme and sought to do him harm. With Joseph the similarity is the way the Prophet's "brothers" from Quraysh declared war on him and wanted to destroy him, but the ultimate outcome was good for him. We can see this in the reports about the conquest of Makkah, when the Prophet (S) said to Quraysh: "I say to you what Joseph said: 'Let no reproach be (cast) on you.'" [Yūsuf 12:92]

With Idrīs the comparison is the high status in the sight of Allah which both attained. With Aaron it is how his people came back to loving him after harming him. With Moses it is how he dealt with his people, as can be seen from the Prophet's (S) statement: "Moses was troubled with more than this, but he bore it with patience."

Ibn Abī Jumrah said: "The reason why Adam was in the first heaven was because he was the first Prophet and the first father, the origin: so he was the first Prophet in the first heaven. Jesus was in the second heaven because he was the closest in time to Muḥammad (S). Joseph was in the third heaven, because the *Ummah* of Muhammad (S) will enter Paradise in his likeness. (i.e. their appearance will be very beautiful.) Idrīs was in the fourth heaven because Allah SWT said: "And We raised him to a lofty station" [Maryam 19:57], and the fourth heaven is exactly in the middle of the seven heavens. Aaron was in the fifth heaven because of his closeness to his brother Moses. Moses was raised above him (in the sixth heaven) by virtue of the fact that he spoke with Allah SWT. The status of Abraham, the Friend of Allah, had to be the highest, but the status of Muḥammad (S), the Beloved of Allah, was higher still, so the Prophet (S) was taken up from the position of Abraham until he was "At a distance of but two bow-lengths or (even) nearer." [al-Najm 53:9]

THE PROPHET MUḤAMMAD'S (S) MEETING WITH OTHER PROPHETS IN HEAVEN

There are some differences as to the state of the Prophets when the Prophet Muḥammad (S) met them on the night of the Isrā'. Were they brought physically to meet the Prophet (S) on that night, or did their souls remain in the places in heaven where the Prophet (S) met them, and take on the form of their bodies, as Abu'l-Wafā' ibn 'Aqīl claims? Some of our greatest scholars favour the first suggestion, that the Prophets were present in body and soul, basing their claim on the *Hadīth* of Anas narrated by Muslim, in which the Prophet (S) said: "On the night of the Isrā' I saw Moses standing and praying in his grave." These scholars say that this indicates that Moses was taken to meet the Prophet (S) after the Prophet (S) had passed by his grave. But this author thinks that this is not necessarily the case. There could be some kind of link between his soul in heaven and his body in the grave on earth. In that case, he would be able to pray whilst his soul remained in heaven.

Anas' report transmitted from Abu Dharr caused some confusion, because Anas said: "(Abu Dharr mentioned that the Prophet (S)) met Adam, Idrīs, Moses, Jesus and Abraham in heaven, but he did not mention their positions, except for two of them. He said that the Prophet (S) met Adam in the first heaven and Abraham in the sixth heaven."

Al-Ḥāfiẓ said: "The majority of reports – apart from these two – prove that Abraham was in the seventh heaven." If we were to accept the idea that the Mi'rāj happened more than once, there is no contradiction, but the majority of reports are more likely to be correct, because they say that the Prophet (S) saw Abraham leaning his back against Bayt al-Ma'mūr, which is undoubtedly in the seventh heaven. A report from 'Ali says that it is in the sixth heaven, near the tree of Ṭūbā. If this report were proven to be authentic, it could be understood to refer to the house which is in the sixth heaven, near the tree of Ṭūbā, because another report from 'Ali says that in every heaven there is a House parallel to the Ka'bah, and each House is filled with angels.

Al-Ḥāfiẓ said: "Qutādah's report from Anas from Mālik ibn Ṣa'ṣa'ah agrees with Thābit's report from Anas in Muslim's *Ṣaḥīḥ*, that Adam was in the first heaven, John and Jesus were in the second heaven, Joseph was in the third heaven, Idris was in the fourth heaven, Aaron was in the fifth heaven, Moses was in the sixth heaven, and Abraham was in the seventh heaven."

MOSES' WEEPING WHEN HE SAW THE STATUS OF THE PROPHET (S)

According to report of Malik ibn Ṣa'ṣa'ah, Moses said: "I weep because of a young man sent after me, whose *Ummah* will enter Paradise in greater numbers than mine." According to a *Ḥadīth* of Abū Sa'īd, Moses said: "The people of Israel claim that I am the most favoured by Allah, but this man is more favoured than me."

According to a report of Abū 'Ubaydah ibn 'Abd Allah ibn Mas'ūd, narrated from his father: 'The Prophet (S) passed by Moses, who said loudly, "You have honoured him and favoured him!" Gabriel said, "This is Moses." The Prophet (S) said, "Who is he complaining to?" Gabriel said, "To his Lord." The Prophet (S) asked, "To his Lord?" Gabriel said, "His Lord knows him."'

The scholars said Moses did not weep out of envy – God forbid! – for in that world envy is removed from every ordinary believer – so how should it be for one who was specially chosen by Allah! Moses wept out of sorrow. This was because so many of his *Ummah* had been disobedient and lost their reward, which led to the loss of his reward, as every Prophet receives reward for everyone who follows him. The number of people in his nation who followed him was less than the number of those who followed our Prophet (S), although the *Ummah* of Moses had been in existence for much longer.

The expression "young man" (*ghulām*) in Anas' report from Malik ibn Ṣa'ṣa'ah is not used in any depreciatory sense, but rather to praise the power and generosity of Allah SWT, because He gave something to the Prophet (S) at that age which He had never before given to anyone older than him.

Moses showed greater concern for this *Ummah*, as regards prayer, than any other Prophet. We can see this in the *Ḥadīth* of Abu Hurayrah, narrated by al-Ṭabarī and al-Bazār, in which the Prophet (S) said: "Moses was the strictest of them towards me when I passed by him, and the best of them to me when I returned." In the *Ḥadīth* of Abū Sa'īd, the Prophet (S) said: " . . . When I returned, I passed by Moses. He is the best friend you have, for he asked me: 'How much has your Lord enjoined upon you?' . . . "

Ibn Abī Jumrah said: "Allah SWT made the Prophets more merciful than other men, hence Moses wept out of mercy towards his *Ummah*." The expression "this young man" refers to the fact that the Prophet (S) was young in relation to the other Prophets. Al-Khaṭṭābī said: "The Arabs call any older man *Ghulām* ("young man") as long as he has any strength left."

It seems to me that Moses was referring to the blessing which Allah had bestowed upon our Prophet (S), namely that his strength continued into middle age, and that when he entered old age no signs of ageing appeared on his body, nor did his strength decrease. When he entered Madīnah – according to Bukhārī's report from the *Ḥadīth* of Anas – and the people saw him making Abū Bakr ride behind him, they called him the youth (*shabāb*) and Abu Bakr the old man (*shaykh*), despite the fact that he was older than Abu Bakr. And Allah knows best.

Al-Qurṭabī said: "The reason why the Prophet (S) referred to Moses with regard to the prayer could be because prayers were enjoined upon Moses' *Ummah* which were not enjoined upon any other, and it was difficult for them. So Moses was worried lest something similar happen to the *Ummah* of Muḥammad (S). This can be seen in his expression: 'I have tried the people before you . . . '"

Other scholars suggest that it may have been because no other Prophet had had more followers, a greater Book or more rules than Moses, so in this respect he was comparable to the Prophet (S). Hence it is appropriate that Moses should wish for similar blessings without desiring any loss for the Prophet (S), and offer advice to him.

Al-Suhaylī said: "It could be because Moses had previously been shown the attributes of the *Ummah* which was to come (i.e. that of Muḥammad (S)), and had asked Allah to make him one of them. In his compassion for them it was as if he was one of them."

THE MUCH-FREQUENTED HOUSE

According to Bukhari's report from Malik ibn Ṣa'ṣa'ah, the Prophet (S) said: "When I entered, there was Abraham. Gabriel said, 'This is your father, greet him.' So I greeted him, and he returned the greeting, then said, 'Welcome to the righteous son and the righteous Prophet.' Then I was taken up to the Lote-tree beyond which none may pass; its fruits were like the pitchers of Hajar, and its leaves were like the ears of elephants. Gabriel said, 'This is the Lote-tree beyond which none may pass.' And there were four rivers, two hidden and two visible. I asked, 'What is this, O Gabriel?' He said: 'The two hidden rivers are rivers in Paradise. The two visible rivers are the Nile and the Euphrates.' Then I was taken up to the Much-Frequented House . . . "

Elsewhere, Bukhari narrates: " . . . We came to the seventh heaven. A voice asked, 'Who is there?' Gabriel answered, 'Gabriel.' The voice asked, 'Who is with you?' Gabriel answered, 'Muḥammad.' The voice asked, 'Has revelation been sent to him? . . . Welcome to him; blessed is the one who has come.' There I found Abraham, so I greeted him, and he said, 'Welcome to you, the best son and the best Prophet.' Then I was taken up to the Much-Frequented House. I asked Gabriel about it, and he said, 'This is the Much-Frequented House. Every day seventy thousand angels pray in it, and when they leave another seventy thousand come.'"

Bukhārī narrated another *Ḥadīth* from Qutādah via Sa'īd ibn Abī 'Urūbah, in which he said: "The Prophet (S) told us: 'The Much-Frequented House is a mosque in heaven, parallel to the Ka'bah. If it were to fall, it would fall onto the Ka'bah. Every day seventy thousand angels enter it, and when they leave, another seventy thousand come.'"

Isḥāq, in his book *al-Musnad*, al-Ṭabarī and others, transmitted a report from 'Ali via Khālid ibn 'Ar'arah, which says that when the Prophet (S) was asked about the "Canopy Raised High" [*al-Saqf al-Marfū'*; cf. al-Ṭūr 52:5], he said: "It is the heaven", and when asked about the "Much-Frequented House" [*al-Bayt al-Ma'mūr*, cf. 52:4], he said: "It is a House in heaven which reflects the Ka'bah. Its sanctity in heaven is like the sanctity of the Ka'bah on earth. Every day seventy thousand angels enter it, and when they leave another seventy thousand come." Al-Ṭabarī added, in his report, that the one who asked these questions was Abd Allah ibn al Kawwā.

THE LOTE-TREE BEYOND WHICH NONE MAY PASS

The reason why it is called "the Lote-tree beyond which none may pass" (*al-Muntahā* lit. = utmost limit) is given in the *Ḥadīth* as Mas'ūd narrated by Muslim: "(Gabriel) took me up as far as the Lote-tree, beyond which none may pass, which is in the sixth heaven. Anything which comes up from earth stops there and is taken from there, and anything which comes down from the region beyond stops there."

Al-Nawawī said: "It is called the Lote-tree beyond which none may pass because the knowledge of the angels stops there: no-one has gone beyond it except the Prophet (S)."

Al-Qurṭabī said in *al-Mufahham*: "The *Ḥadīth* of Anas would seem to indicate that it is in the seventh heaven, because after mentioning the seventh heaven, the Prophet (S) said: "Then he took me up to the Lote-tree . . . " The *Ḥadīth* of Ibn Mas'ūd states that it was in the sixth heaven. This is undoubtedly a contradiction, but Anas' statement is favoured by the majority. Anas' *Ḥadīth* states clearly that the Lote-tree is the point where the knowledge of every Prophet and angel ends, according to Ka'b's statement. Whatever is beyond the Lote-tree is hidden and known only to Allah SWT, and who has more knowledge than He?

According to the *Ḥadīth* of Abū Dharr, it was "veiled in colours indescribable." According to report of Thābit from Anas, narrated by Muslim, "When it was veiled with whatever it was veiled with by the command of Allah, it changed, and no creature of Allah can describe it because it is so beautiful."

Ibn Daḥyah said: "The Lote-tree alone was chosen, because it has three attributes: extensive shade, delicious food and beautiful scent. These attributes symbolize faith, which combines speech, actions and intentions. The shade represents action, the food represents intention and the scent represents speech."

THE RIVERS SEEN BY THE PROPHET (S)

According to Malik ibn Ṣa'ṣa'ah's report, narrated by Bukhārī: "(Gabriel) said, 'This is the Lote-tree beyond which none may pass.' There were four rivers, two hidden and two visible. I asked, 'What is this, O Gabriel?' He said, 'The two hidden rivers are rivers in Paradise. The two visible rivers are the Nile and the Euphrates.'"

Another report from Malik says: "At the foot of the Lote-tree were four rivers."

According to Sharīk's report: "There were two rivers running through the first heaven. The Prophet (S) asked, 'What are these two rivers, O Gabriel?' Gabriel answered: 'They are the essence of the Nile and Euphrates.' Then Gabriel took him through the first heaven, where they saw another river, above which stood a castle made of pearls and chrysolite. The Prophet (S) struck it with his hand and saw that it was pungent musk. He asked, 'What is this, O Gabriel?' Gabriel answered, 'This is al-Kawthar, which your Lord is keeping for you' . . . "

Al-Ḥāfiẓ said: "Muslim transmitted a *Ḥadīth* of Abu Hurayrah which said: 'Four of the rivers in Paradise are: the Nile, the Euphrates, Sīḥān and Jīḥān.'"

Ibn Abī Ḥāṭim transmitted a report of Yazīd ibn Abī Malik, from Anas, which says: "After the Prophet (S) mentioned that he had seen Abraham, he said: 'Then (Gabriel) took me up beyond the seventh heaven, until we reached a river on which stood tents made of pearls, sapphires and chrysolite and above which were green birds – the most beautiful birds I have ever seen. Gabriel said, 'This is al-Kawthar, which Allah has given to you.' In the river were vessels of gold and silver; it ran over pebbles of sapphire and chrysolite, and its water was whiter than milk. I took one of the vessels, scooped up some of that water and drank it. It was sweeter than honey and had a scent more beautiful than that of musk.'"

It was suggested that the Nile and Euphrates were described as rivers of Paradise because they resemble the rivers of Paradise in that they are so sweet, so beautiful and so blessed. And Allah knows best.

ALLAH'S GUIDING THE PROPHET (S) TO THE FITRAH (NATURAL DISPOSITION)

Bukhārī narrated from the *Ḥadīth* of Abū Hurayrah: "On the night of the Isrā', whilst he was in Jerusalem, two vessels – one containing wine, the other milk – were brought to the Prophet (S). He looked at them, then chose the milk. Gabriel said, 'Praise be to Allah, who has guided you to the *Fiṭrah*. If you had chosen the wine, your *Ummah* would have died.'"

According to the *Ḥadīth* of Malik ibn Ṣa'ṣa'ah: ". . . Then I was taken up to the Much-Frequented House. I was presented with three vessels, containing wine, milk and honey. I chose the milk, so (Gabriel) said, 'This is the natural disposition (*Fiṭrah*) of your *Ummah*.'"

According to a *Ḥadīth* transmitted by Anas ibn Mālik, the Prophet (S) said: "I was taken up to the Lote-tree, where I saw four rivers: two visible and two hidden. The two visible rivers were the Nile and Euphrates, and the two hidden rivers were rivers of Paradise. I was presented with three vessels, containing milk, honey and wine. I chose the one which contained milk, and drank it. I was told: "You have chosen the *Fiṭrah* of yourself and your *Ummah*."

Al-Qurṭabī suggested that the reason why milk was described as the *Fiṭrah* could be because it is the first food of the new-born child. The reason why the Prophet (S) took the milk and nothing else could be because he was used to it, and because it causes no physical damage.

A *Ḥadīth* of Abū Hurayrah, narrated by Ibn 'Ā'idh, mentions that the Prophet (S) saw Abraham, then goes on to say: "Then we set off, and we were brought three covered vessels. Gabriel said, 'O Muḥammad, will you not drink of what your Lord has provided for you?' So I took one of the vessels, and found it contained honey.

I drank a little of it, then took another vessel, which contained milk. I drank it until my thirst was quenched. Gabriel said, 'Will you not drink from the third vessel?' I said, 'I have already drunk my fill.' He said, 'May Allah guide you.' "

Muslim also narrates a report from Anas via Thābit, which states that the vessels were brought to the Prophet (S) in Bayt al-Maqdis, before the Mi'rāj: "Then I entered the mosque, prayed two Rak'at, and came out. Gabriel brought me a vessel of wine and a vessel of milk. I chose the milk. Gabriel said, 'You have chosen the *Fiṭrah*.' Then he was taken up to heaven."

According to the *Ḥadīth* of Shaddād ibn Aws: "I prayed in the mosque as much as Allah willed, and I was seized with a great thirst, such as I had never known. Two vessels were brought to me: one of milk and one of honey. I was trying to decide between them, then Allah guided me and I chose the milk. An old man in front of me said to Gabriel, 'Your companion has chosen the *Fiṭrah*.' "

Ibn Isḥāq narrates a *Ḥadīth* of Abu Sa'īd concerning the story of the Isrā': "The Prophet (S) led them (i.e. the Prophets) in prayer, then three vessels were brought to him: one of milk, one of wine, and one of water – and he chose the milk . . ."

There are some differences as to where the Prophet (S) was presented with these vessels. It could be that he was presented with them twice: once in Jerusalem after he had completed his prayers, and became very thirsty, and then at the Lote-tree when he saw the four rivers and again became thirsty.

There are also differences as to the number of vessels and their contents. It has been suggested that some narrators mentioned what others omitted, so in total there were four vessels, containing four different substances, drawn from the four rivers which the Prophet (S) saw flowing from beneath the Lote-tree.

A *Ḥadīth* of Abū Hurayrah, narrated by al-Ṭabarī, mentions the Lote-tree and says: "Flowing from beneath it were rivers of sweet water, fresh milk, delicious wine and pure honey." This could mean that the Prophet (S) was shown a vessel drawn from each river. A report narrated from Ka'b adds: "The river of honey is the Nile, the river of milk is Jīḥān, the river of wine is the Euphrates, and the river of water is Sīḥān." And Allah knows best.

Ibn al-Munīr said: "No reason is given for the Prophet's (S) leaving the honey to take the milk, as was given for his leaving the wine. It could be that milk is more nutritious, it strengthens the bones and muscles, and by itself can be a complete 'food'. Drinking milk contains no element of extravagance, indeed it is more akin to asceticism. Honey may be *Ḥalāl*, but it is one of the pleasures of which one fears that those who enjoy it may be included among those of whom the Qur'ān warns that it will be said to them: 'Ye received your good things in the life of the world . . . '" [al-Aḥqāf 46:20]

The reason why the Prophet (S) chose the milk could be that he became thirsty – as mentioned above – and milk would quench his thirst better than wine or honey. His thirst could be the reason why he chose the milk, but it happened to be better in other respects as well. Ibn al-Munīr said: "This does not contradict the *Aḥādīth* which state that the Prophet (S) loved sweets and honey, because although he was very fond of them, he did not eat them to excess."

ADDITIONAL DETAILS NOT GIVEN BY BUKHĀRĪ

Muslim narrates a *Ḥadīth* from Anas via Qutādah and Hammām: "Whilst I was walking in Paradise, I came upon a river whose banks were hollow domes of pearls, and whose mud was pungent musk. Gabriel said, 'This is al-Kawthar.'"

Ibn Abī Ḥāṭim and Ibn 'Ā'idh both narrated from Anas via Yazīd ibn Abī Mālik: "Then we set off until we reached the Lote-tree, and I was veiled with clouds of every colour. Gabriel stood back, and I prostrated myself." According to a *Ḥadīth* of Ibn Mas'ūd narrated by Muslim: "The Prophet (S) was given the command to pray five times daily, the final *Āyāt* of Surat al-Baqarah were revealed, and the major sins of every one of his *Ummah* who does not associate partners with Allah were forgiven." The same report also adds: "Then the clouds were removed from me, Gabriel took my hand and we left quickly. I met Abraham, who did not say anything. Then I met Moses, who asked, 'What happened?' . . . The Prophet (S) asked Gabriel, 'Why is it that everyone in heaven welcomed me and smiled at me, except for one man? I greeted him, and he returned the greeting and welcomed me, but he did not smile at me.' Gabriel said, 'O Muhammad, that was Malik, the gatekeeper of Hell. He has never smiled since he was created, and if he were to smile at anyone, he would have smiled at you.'"

According to a *Ḥadīth* of Ḥudhayfah narrated by Aḥmad and Tirmidhī: "The gates of heaven were opened for them, and they saw Paradise and Hell, and all the promises of the Hereafter." According to a *Ḥadīth* of Abū Sa'īd: "He was shown Paradise; its pomegranates were like buckets and its birds were like camels. Then he was shown Hell-fire; if stones and iron were thrown into it, it would devour them."

Ibn Abī Ḥāṭim narrated from Anas via Yazīd ibn Abī Malik: "Gabriel said: 'O Muhammad, have you asked your Lord to show you the Companions, with big beautiful, and lustrous eyes?' [*al-Hūr al-'Ayn*, cf. al-Ṭūr 52:20]. He said, 'Yes'. Gabriel said, 'Go to those women and greet them.' So he went in and greeted them, and they returned the greeting. Then he asked: 'Who are you?' They said: 'Fair (Companions), good, beautiful' . . . " [al-Raḥmān 55:70]

According to a report narrated by Abū 'Ubaydah ibn 'Abd Allah ibn Mas'ūd from his father: "Abraham said to the Prophet (S): 'O Prophet, you are going to meet your Lord tonight. Your *Ummah* is the last and the weakest, so if you are able to ask anything of your Lord, beseech Him on behalf of your *Ummah*.' "

A report narrated by al-Wāqidi says: "The Prophet (S) used to ask his Lord to show him Paradise and Hell. On Saturday, the seventeenth day of Ramaḍān, eighteen months before the Hijrah, whilst he was sleeping in his house at noon, Gabriel and Michael came to him and said: 'Let us go to that which you have asked for.' They took him to the area between al-Maqām and Zamzam, and the Mi'rāj ('ladder') was brought to him – it was the most beautiful sight. They took him up into heaven, where he met the Prophets, then reached the Lote-tree, beyond which none may pass. He saw Paradise and Hell, and the five daily prayers were enjoined upon him." If this report were proven, it would obviously be referring to another Mi'rāj, because it says that it was noon, and the Mi'rāj took place from Makkah. Thus, it contradicts the *Ṣaḥīḥ* reports on two points, and also it says that prayer was enjoined on that occasion. It has been suggested that the Mi'rāj took place a second time, or that the first one was a dream and this took place whilst the Prophet (S) was awake – or vice versa. And Allah knows best.

DID THE PROPHET (S) SEE HIS LORD ON THE NIGHT OF THE ISRA'?

Sharīk's report, quoted above, says: " . . . Then Gabriel took him higher, to regions which are unknown to all except Allah, until they reached the Lote-tree, beyond which none may pass. Then Allah the Almighty drew near, until He was very close indeed, and revealed the commandment: 'Fifty prayers, day and night, are prescribed for your *Ummah*.' . . . "

Bukhārī narrates that Masrūq said: "I asked 'Āishah, 'O Mother, did Muḥammad (S) see his Lord?' She said, 'What you say makes my hair stand on end. I shall tell you three things, which if anyone says they are true, he is a liar. If anyone tells you that Muḥammad (S) saw his Lord, he is lying.' Then she recited: 'No vision can grasp Him, but His grasp is over all vision: He is above all comprehension, yet is acquainted with all things' [al-An'ām 6:103], and 'It is not fitting for a man that God should speak to him except by inspiration or from behind a veil . . . ' [al-Shūrā 42:51]. Then she went on to say: 'Whoever tells you that the Prophet knows what will happen tomorrow, he is a liar, . . . Nor does anyone know what it is that he will earn on the morrow . . . [Luqmān 31:34]. Whoever tells you that he concealed anything is a liar: "O Apostle! Proclaim the (Message) which hath been sent to thee from thy Lord . . . " [al-Mā'idah 5:67]. But he saw Gabriel in his true form twice.' "

Al-Khaṭṭābī said that the report which suggested that it was Allah Himself Who drew close contradicts the opinion of the first Muslims, the *'Ulamā'* and the scholars of *Tafsīr*. He gave three suggestions as to the meaning of the phrase: "Then he approached and came closer:" [al-Najm 53:8], viz.:

1. That Gabriel approached Muḥammad (S).

2. That Gabriel came down and approached him after being raised up, so that the Prophet (S) saw him suspended. This was one of the signs of Allah, that He was able to make Gabriel be suspended in the air without any visible means of support or having to hold on to anything.
3. That Gabriel approached and Muḥammad (S) prostrated himself before his Lord, giving thanks for what He had given him.

The phrase "he saw him" means that the Prophet (S) saw Gabriel, with six hundred wings. Al-Bayhaqī transmitted a similar report from Abū Hurayrah. Al-Khaṭṭābī said that all these reports agree that the Prophet (S) saw Gabriel, but the *Āyah* "So did he convey the inspiration to his servant" (conveyed) what he (meant) to convey [al-Najm 53:10] would seem to contradict it. Al-Ḥasan suggested that the noun *'Abd* (= servant) referred to Gabriel, i.e. that Allah inspired Gabriel. But al-Farrā' suggested that it meant that Allah conveyed the inspiration to His servant Muḥammad (S) which He meant to convey.

Those scholars who favour the idea that it was Allah Himself Who approached have tried to offer various explanations. For example, al-Qāḍī 'Ayyāḍ said, in *al-Shifā'*, that describing Allah as approaching and drawing nigh did not imply a literal approach in space and time, but a metaphorical approach, to confirm the high status of His Prophet Muhammad (S) and to honour him. It may be likened to the expressions in the *Ḥadīth*: "Allah descends to the first heaven", and in the *Ḥadīth* Qudsi: " . . . Whoever draws near to Me a hand's span, I draw near to him an arm's length."

'Ā'ISHAH DENIED THAT THE PROPHET (S) SAW HIS LORD

This was proven in *Ṣaḥīḥ Muslim*, in a report narrated from Masrūq via al-Sha'bi and Dāwūd ibn Abī Hind. "I said: Did not Allah SWT say: 'For indeed he saw him at a second descent?' [al-Najm 53:13] 'Ā'ishah said, 'I was the first person of this *Ummah* to put this question to the Prophet (S), and he said, "That was Gabriel."' Another version of this *Ḥadīth* narrated by Ibn Mardawayh says: "A'ishah said: 'I was the first person of this *Ummah* to put this question to the Prophet (S). I asked him, 'O Messenger of Allah, did you see your Lord?' He answered, 'No, I only saw Gabriel descending.'"

'Ā'ishah's opinion differs from that of Ibn 'Abbās. Al-Tirmidhī narrates a report from Ibn 'Abbās via 'Ikramah and al-Ḥakam ibn Abān, which says that Ibn 'Abbās said: "Muḥammad saw his Lord." 'Ikramah asked: "But didn't Allah SWT say: 'No vision can grasp Him . . . '" [al-An 'am 6:103]. Ibn 'Abbās said: "Woe to you! That means that no vision could grasp Him if He appeared in His own light. But the Prophet (S) saw him twice."

The *Āyah* means that the Prophet (S) could not see Allah completely, but it does not imply that he did not see Him at all.

Al-Qurṭabī said: 'It is proven in the Qur'ān that Allah SWT could be seen by one of His creation:

> "Verily, from (the Light of) their Lord, that Day, will they be veiled." (al-Muṭaffifin 83:15).'

This *Āyah* refers to the disbelievers:

> "Some faces, that Day, will beam (in brightness and beauty) – looking towards their Lord; . . . " (al-Qiyāmah 75:22-3)

If it is possible for men to see Allah in the Hereafter, it must also be possible in this life, as the two are the same for Allah.

'Ayyāḍ said: "It is quite possible that man may see Allah SWT, and there are well-known, authentic reports which prove that the believers will see Him in the Hereafter. But concerning this life, Malik said: 'Man cannot see Allah in this life, because Allah is Eternal, and the Eternal cannot be seen by the finite. But in the Hereafter, when the Believers have been given their eternal vision, the Eternal will be seen by eternal beings.'" 'Ayyāḍ said: "This idea means that it is impossible for man to see Allah in this life only because he is not capable of beholding Him. But if Allah wants to make it possible for any of His servants to see Him, then He is able to do so."

A *Ḥadīth* in *Ṣaḥīḥ Muslim* proves this difference between this life and the Hereafter: "Know that none of you will see your Lord until you die." Ibn Khazīmah reported it from the *Ḥadīths* of Abū Amāmah and 'Ubādah ibn al-Ṣāmit. Even if it were logically possible for man to see Allah in this life, it has not been proven in any *Ḥadīth* narrated from the Prophet (S). But those who favour the idea that the Prophet (S) did see his Lord in this life could argue that the speaker does not necessarily include himself in his general statements.

THE OPINIONS OF THE FIRST GENERATION

The first generation of Muslims differed as to whether the Prophet (S) saw his Lord. 'Ā'ishah and Ibn Mas'ūd said that he did not; they differed from Abū Dharr and others who said that he did see Him. 'Abd al-Razzāq transmitted a report from Mu'ammar, stating that al-Ḥasan swore that Muḥammad had seen his Lord.

Ibn Khazīmah narrated a report from 'Urwah ibn al-Zubayr to prove it, and he used to become angry if anyone mentioned that 'Ā'ishah had denied it. The students of Ibn 'Abbās all suggested it, and Ka'b al-Aḥbār and al-Zuhrī, along with his companions, Mu'ammar and others, were all sure of it. This was also the suggestion favoured by al-Ash'arī and most of his followers, but later they differed as to whether the Prophet (S) had seen Allah with his eyes or his heart.

Various reports were transmitted by Ibn 'Abbās, some general and some specific. We must understand the general reports in the light of the specific. For example, al-Nisā'i transmitted a *Ṣaḥīḥ* report from Ibn 'Abbās via 'Ikramah, according to which 'Ikramah asked: "Did Muḥammad see his Lord?", and Ibn 'Abbās sent word to him to say that he had indeed seen Him. Muslim narrated a *Ḥadīth* from Ibn 'Abbās via Abu'l-'Āliyah, concerning the *Āyah*:

> "The (Prophet's) (mind and) heart in no way falsified that which he saw." (al-Najm 53:11)

Ibn 'Abbās said: "He saw his Lord with his heart twice." A report narrated by Ibn Mardawayh from Ibn 'Abbās via 'Aṭā' explains it further: "The Prophet (S) did not see Him with his eyes, but with his heart."

On this basis, we may reconcile between Ibn 'Abbās' affirmation and 'Ā'ishah's denial by saying that it is possible that 'Ā'ishah was denying that the Prophet (S) saw Allah with his eyes, whilst Ibn 'Abbās was affirming that he saw Him with his heart.

Ibn Khazīmah narrated a report with a strong *Isnād* from Anas, who said: "Muḥammad saw his Lord." Muslim narrates a *Ḥadīth* of Abū Dharr according to which he asked the Prophet (S) about this, and the Prophet (S) said: "There was so much Light – how could I see Him?" Aḥmad also narrates a *Ḥadīth* from Abū Dharr, according to which the Prophet (S) said: "I saw Light." Ibn Khazīmah narrates from Abū Dharr: "(The Prophet (S)) saw Him with his heart, not with his eyes." This could explain what Abu Dharr meant when he mentioned Light; namely that the Light prevented him from seeing Allah with his eyes.

Al-Qurṭabī preferred not to seek further clarification of this matter, and attributed this opinion to a group of scholars. He strengthened it further by stating that there is no definitive evidence concerning this matter. The evidence claimed by the supporters of either opinion is inconsistent, and can be interpreted in several ways. Al-Qurṭabī said: "This question does not deal with practical matters; it has to do with beliefs, so we would need strong evidence to settle the matter. As we have no strong evidence, we should not delve too deeply into the matter."

Ibn Khazīmah favours the idea that the Prophet (S) did indeed see Allah, and presents a great deal of evidence which we cannot quote here for lack of space.

On the basis of the reports from Ibn 'Abbās, he suggests that the Prophet (S) saw his Lord twice – once with his eyes and once with his heart.

One of those who claimed that our Prophet (S) saw his Lord was Imām Aḥmad. Al-Khallāl narrated from al-Mazūrī: "I said to Aḥmad, 'They say that 'Ā'ishah said: "Whoever claims that Muḥammad saw his Lord has uttered a grave slander against Allah." How can we reject what she said?' Aḥmad said: 'The Prophet (S) said: "I saw my Lord" – and the Prophet's words carry more weight than those of 'Ā'ishah.'"

Ibn Qayyim al-Jawziyyah rebuked those who claimed that Aḥmad has said: "(The Prophet (S)) saw his Lord with his eyes", and said that Ahmad on one occasion said: "Muḥammad saw his Lord", and on another occasion he said: "That the Prophet (S) saw his Lord with his heart." Some of the later scholars said that the Prophet (S) saw his Lord with his eyes, but this is an embellishment added by the narrator of the *Hadīth*.

CONCLUSION

The generally-accepted view is that the Isrā' and Mi'rāj occurred on the same night, and took place when the Prophet (S) was awake, not in a dream. The Prophet (S) travelled physically, not metaphorically.

During his ascent to heaven, he met with earlier Prophets and saw some of the features of that other world. At this time the daily prayers were enjoined upon the Muslim *Ummah*, and, according to many scholars, the Prophet (S) saw his Lord.

GLOSSARY

Aḥādīth: The plural of *Ḥadīth*.

Al-Kawthar: A River or Pool in Paradise.

Āyah: A verse of the Holy Qur'ān.

Bayt al-Maqdis: The name used for Jerusalem and in particular for the Mosque from which the Prophet Muḥammad (S) ascended to Heaven.

Fiṭrah: Man's true nature.

Fiqh: The science of understanding the rules governing the performance of Islamic duties.

Ḥadīth: A direct report of what the prophet Muḥammad (S) said or did.

Halal: That which is lawful in Islam.

Hijrah: The migration of the Prophet (S) from Makkah to Madinah. The start of the Muslim calendar.

Ijmā: The consensus of the Ulama' and the Ummah.

Isnād: The chain of narrators of a *Ḥadīth*.

Isrā': The Prophet Muḥammad's (S) journey from Makkah to Jerusalem.

Mi'rāj: The Prophet Muḥammad's (S) ascension to Heaven.

Qiblah: The direction in which a Muslim must face when they pray. Jerusalem was the first Qiblah, later it was changed to the Ka'bah in Makkah.

Ṣaḥīḥ: Used to refer to the most authentic books of *Ḥadīth*.

Ṣalāt: The five prescribed daily prayers of the Muslims.

Siddīq: Trustworthy – here it refers to Abu Bakr.

Tafsīr: A commentary on the Qur'ān or *Ḥadīth*.

'Ulamā': The learned men of Qur'ān, Fiqh and Ḥadīth studies.

Ummah: The Muslim People – followers of Prophet Muḥammad (S) or true followers of the Prophets before Prophet Muḥammad (S).

Zamzam: The ancient well situated about thirty yards east of the Ka'bah, first found by Prophet Ishmael.